MW00682142

PRESENTS

Greetings from Amsterdam

Copyright © 2017 by Stuff Dutch People Like

Published in the Netherlands by Stuff Dutch People Like

Some of the material in this book may have originally appeared in different form, on the popular blog **StuffDutchPeopleLike.com**

Photo & other credits can be found on page 246

ISBN 978–90–828620–0–3

Printed in the EU

10 9 8 7 6 5 4 3 2 1

www.stuffdutchpeoplelike.com

www.facebook.com/stuffdutchpeoplelike

www.instagram.com/stuffdutchpeoplelike

www.twitter.com/stuffdutchlike

For media inquiries, corporate & volume sales or any other requests, please contact us at **hello@stuffdutchpeoplelike.com**

Contents

– 1 –

Welcome to Amsterdam

Get to know Amsterdam's rich history and diverse culture. Whether you are already here, wandering the city's romantic canals, or are planning a future trip, you'll learn something new, guaranteed!

Amsterdam

Ever wanted to explore a city rich in art, culture, and a history that spans centuries? Welcome to Amsterdam, one of the most interesting and beautiful cities in the world. Take a romantic trip along the canals, visit one of the many museums including the famous Anne Frank House, or pop into one of the bars or restaurants to sample Amsterdam's diverse cuisine. Alternatively, you could hire a bicycle and see streets lined with architecture from the Dutch Golden Age, statues, and ancient market squares—all with the wind in your hair. Whatever the reason for your visit, feel free to immerse yourself in this unique and delightful city which has plenty to offer.

ECONOMY

Amsterdam has a thriving and diversified economy. Since its Golden Age days as a major trading hub, Amsterdam has retained its status as a global center of commerce and today is home to many international corporations and institutions.

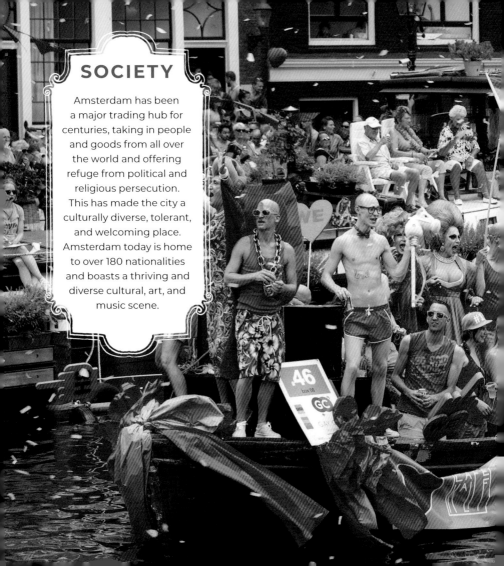

SOCIETY

Amsterdam has been a major trading hub for centuries, taking in people and goods from all over the world and offering refuge from political and religious persecution. This has made the city a culturally diverse, tolerant, and welcoming place. Amsterdam today is home to over 180 nationalities and boasts a thriving and diverse cultural, art, and music scene.

BICYCLES

What makes Amsterdam truly unique is its cycling culture. You will see people of all ages using a bicycle as their primary mode of transportation. From busy mothers to CEO's—and even the mayor—cycling is deeply ingrained into Amsterdam life. There are close to 1 million bicycles in Amsterdam, with many Amsterdammers owning more than one bike. Cycling infrastructure is unbeatable with over 400km of bicycle paths. Fun fact: Every year, close to 15,000 bicycles have to be fished from the canals!

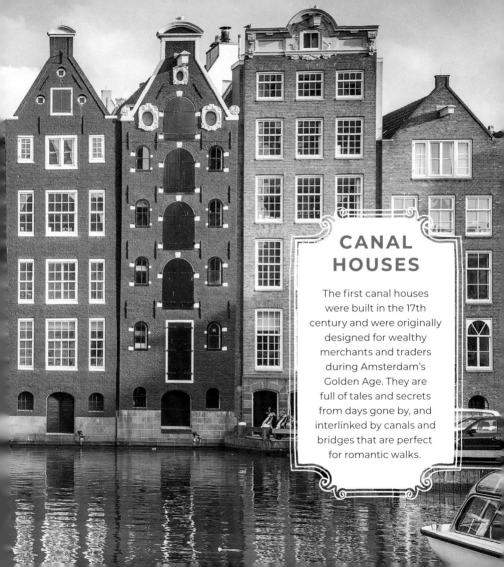

CANAL HOUSES

The first canal houses were built in the 17th century and were originally designed for wealthy merchants and traders during Amsterdam's Golden Age. They are full of tales and secrets from days gone by, and interlinked by canals and bridges that are perfect for romantic walks.

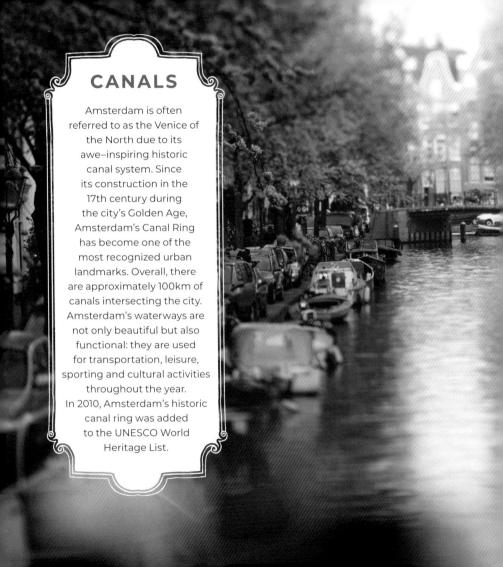

CANALS

Amsterdam is often referred to as the Venice of the North due to its awe–inspiring historic canal system. Since its construction in the 17th century during the city's Golden Age, Amsterdam's Canal Ring has become one of the most recognized urban landmarks. Overall, there are approximately 100km of canals intersecting the city. Amsterdam's waterways are not only beautiful but also functional: they are used for transportation, leisure, sporting and cultural activities throughout the year.

In 2010, Amsterdam's historic canal ring was added to the UNESCO World Heritage List.

BRIDGES

Spanning
Amsterdam's canals
are a wide array
of bridges that create a
network, interlacing islands
and joining districts. There
are around 2,500 bridges,
with the oldest thought
to have been created in
1648. The bridges add
a little Venetian romance
to the city and many have
beautiful decorations. The
materials used for bridge
construction vary from
brick to steel and you will
find a wide range
of architects stamping
their mark across
the city.

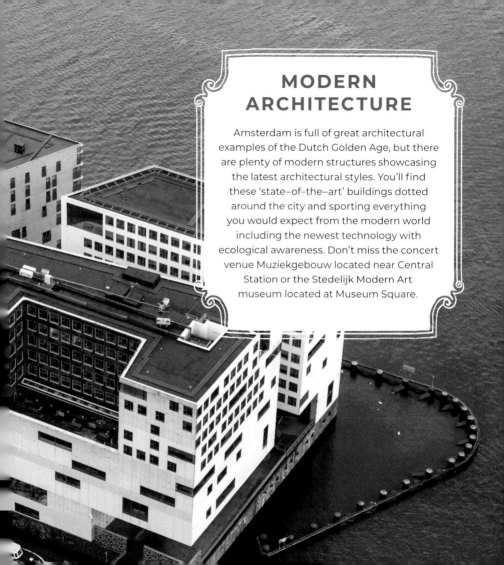

MODERN ARCHITECTURE

Amsterdam is full of great architectural examples of the Dutch Golden Age, but there are plenty of modern structures showcasing the latest architectural styles. You'll find these 'state-of-the-art' buildings dotted around the city and sporting everything you would expect from the modern world including the newest technology with ecological awareness. Don't miss the concert venue Muziekgebouw located near Central Station or the Stedelijk Modern Art museum located at Museum Square.

Het Muziekgebouw
(concert hall)

The Stedelijk
Museum
Of Modern
Art

DELICACIES

The Dutch can lay claim to
several delicacies that have become
popular all around the world. The first
thing you might think of is cheese, but
that is just the tip of the iceberg. There are
many sweet treats to nibble along–side
your coffee and some hearty meals
to keep you satiated throughout
your trip.

STROOP-WAFELS

These caramel filled biscuits are particularly delicious when placed over your hot tea or coffee to warm. The outside is made by baking dough in a waffle maker and thinly slicing it to form a wafer–like biscuit, which is then filled with sweet and sticky caramel syrup.

DUTCH CHEESE

Don't forget to stock up on cheese when visiting Amsterdam. There's plenty to choose from, besides the famous Edam. Leerdammer is a medium hard cheese (with holes) and has a mellow, nutty flavour. Gouda is likely the most popular cheese worldwide and is one of the oldest known cheeses to be recorded. Limburger has a particularly strong smell and Maasdammer is sweet, soft, and nutty.

PANCAKES

Dutch pancakes (pannenkoeken) can be served with sweet or savoury fillings and are a national favourite. They are thinner than American pancakes but not as thin as the French version, crepes. The Dutch like to roll up their pancakes with their filling inside before devouring them!

POFFERTJES

These puffy treats resemble tiny pancakes and have a light, fluffy texture. They are mostly served with powdered sugar and a bit of butter. You will find them sold by many street vendors throughout the city.

DUTCH FRIES

Dutch fries are usually called patat or friet in the Netherlands. What makes them especially noteworthy are the seemingly limitless array of toppings. From mayo, garlic sauce and ketchup, to peanut sauce and chopped onions, you are sure to find something to your liking. Fries may have originated in Belgium but the Dutch have added their seal of approval and a little extra on top!

STAMPPOT

Stamppot roughly translates as 'mash pot' and is the ultimate comfort food, Dutch style. It consists of mashed potatoes and other mashed vegetables. It often includes sauerkraut and onion, and can be topped with smoked sausage. A perfect dish for warming you up on cold winter days.

SNACK CULTURE

Head to FEBO when you're in the market for a savoury/fried treat and you will find automatic dispensers filled with piping hot snacks. The fast food chain was founded in 1941 and has been popular ever since. There are 20 FEBO shops in Amsterdam so you'll never go hungry.

BITTER-BALLEN

Bitterballen are typically a deep–fried pub snack, full of flavour, and are the perfect finger food for a night on the town. They often have a varied content, some being meaty and others just vegetable–based, but all are wrapped in bread crumbs and fried until crispy.

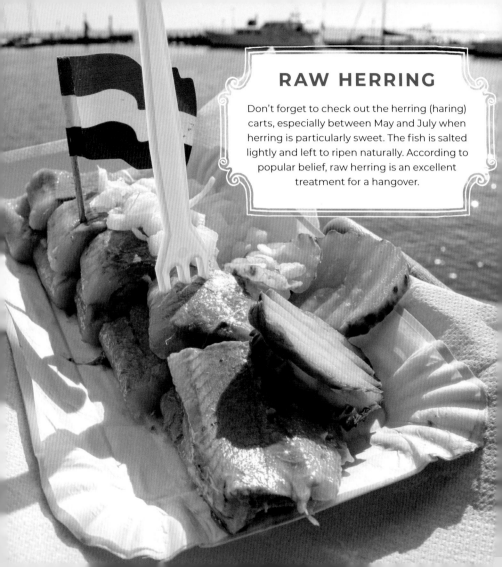

RAW HERRING

Don't forget to check out the herring (haring) carts, especially between May and July when herring is particularly sweet. The fish is salted lightly and left to ripen naturally. According to popular belief, raw herring is an excellent treatment for a hangover.

JENEVER (DUTCH GIN)

Jenever is the juniper–flavored national liquor of the Netherlands from which gin evolved. There are two types of Jenever: oude (old) and jonge (young), based on the distilling techniques used. Young Jenever has a neutral taste, like vodka, while old Jenever has a smoother, more aromatic taste.

– 2 –
History of Amsterdam

Amsterdam has a long-standing history of culture, trade, and commerce. What began as a 13th-century fishing village now is a thriving, cosmopolitan capital city.

1270	Dam built on Amstel River (approximate date).	1631	Artist Rembrandt moves to Jodenbreestraat in Amsterdam.	1838	Artis Zoo opens.
1306	Amsterdam granted city rights.	1638	Hortus Medicus founded.	1840	Coster Diamonds founded.
1425	Singel canal dug.	1642	Rembrandt's artwork *The Night Watch* shown in the Kloveniersdoelen.	1862	Bloemenmarkt (flower market) founded.
1568	Amsterdam supports Catholics in the Dutch Revolt.			1867	Heineken brewery built.
		1652	City Hall burns down.	1870	Amstel Brewery founded.
1585	City expands beyond the Singel.	1655	New City Hall built on Dam Square.	1876	North Sea Canal opens.
1586	Admiralty of Amsterdam formed.	1675	Portuguese Synagogue built.	1881	Telephone in operation.
				1885	Rijksmuseum opens.
1601	Goldsmith's guild established.	1679	Wynand–Fockink in business.	1888	Concertgebouw built, and Royal Concertgebouw Orchestra founded.
1602	Amsterdam Stock Exchange and Dutch East India Company founded.	1682	Begijnhof Chapel and Amstelhof built.	1889	Amsterdam Centraal railway station opens.
		1691	Magere Brug (skinny bridge) built.		
1609	Bank of Amsterdam founded.	1774	Theatre opens on the Leidseplein.	1890	Victoria Hotel, Amsterdam in business.
1613	Grachtengordel (canal ring) development begins.	1774	Population: 217,024	1900	Gemeentetram Amsterdam tramway established.
		1795	French in power.		AFC Ajax football club formed.
1621	Dutch West India Company founded.	1814	Amsterdam becomes capital of the Netherlands.		Population: 523,557.

1903	Beurs van Berlage built.	1960	Anne Frank House museum established on the Prinsengracht.
1911	Rembrandt House Museum opens.		
1915	De Bijenkorf (Amsterdam) department store built.	1961	Amsterdam RAI Exhibition and Convention Centre opens.
1919	Public library opens.	1962	Hilton Hotel in business.
	Population: 647,120.	1973	Van Gogh Museum opens.
1921	Tuschinski cinema built.	1990	Population: 695,221.
1926	HEMA (store) in business on Kalverstraat.	1996	Amsterdam Gay Pride begins.
1928	Summer Olympics held.		Amsterdam Arena built.
1940	German occupation begins.	2000	Prostitution in the Netherlands legalized.
	Het Parool newspaper begins publication.	2001	First legalized same–sex marriage in the Netherlands occurs.
1944	Anne Frank family arrested.		
1945	German occupation ends.	2009	Hermitage Amsterdam opens.
	De Volkskrant newspaper in publication.	2012	EYE Film Institute Netherlands opens.
1947	Anne Frank's Diary published.	2017	Population: 847 129 within city limits (1,351,587 for Amsterdam urban area)
1956	National Monument erected in Dam Square.		

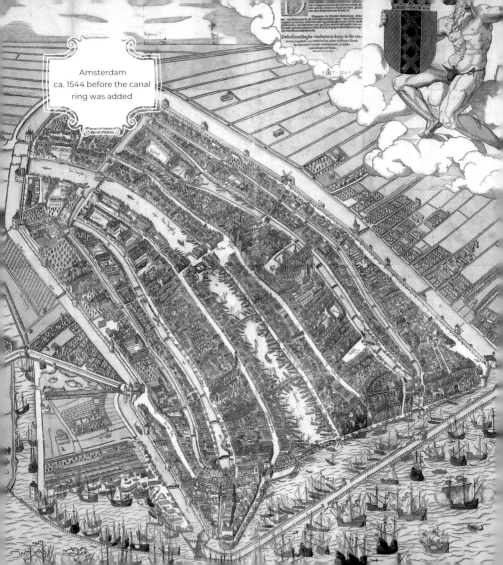

Amsterdam
ca. 1544 before the canal
ring was added

FOUNDING
OF AMSTERDAM

Amsterdam was founded around 1270 on the banks of the river Amstel, but it wasn't until 1306 that it was granted the right to become a city. The word 'Amsterdam' refers to the dam over the river Amstel and in 1425 the first canal was created—thus beginning to shape Amsterdam into the city it now is.

The city was full of unrest during the medieval period due to religious differences between the Protestants and Catholics but after a reform in the early 1500s things began to settle, allowing the city to become more peaceful.

Trade continued, but it wasn't until 1585 that the Golden Age really began. Amsterdam was leading the way in trade far and wide, and had begun to colonize distant lands. As a result, the population increased and, governed by a group of regents, it prospered. Immigration and trade brought many cultures and customs together bringing with it art, music, and many other influential aspects.

GOLDEN AGE

The Golden Age began in 1585 and ended in 1672. With the increase in population due to skilled workers migrating to the Netherlands, an increase of wealth due to good trade and work ethics, and investment in the sciences and arts, Amsterdam thrived like never before.

The decline of the Golden Age was an accumulation of many things including costly wars, political corruption, and political instability throughout Europe.

The Golden Age shaped Amsterdam, and it is evident throughout the city and celebrated in its architecture, galleries, and museums as well as on its canals and streets. You will find portrayals of the Golden Age in Rembrandt's work among others, immortalized on canvas.

THE VOC

The VOC or Dutch East India Company was founded in 1602 and dissolved in 1799. It was created to trade with the far east and was one of the Netherlands' first multinational companies. During the time that it was operational, the company forged alliances and treaties, trade routes, and established colonies and bases. The VOC had a major influence on the identity of Amsterdam and its legacy lives on today.

The Semper
Augustus is
famous for
being the most
expensive tulip
sold during the
tulip mania in the
Netherlands in the
17th century

Semper A

TULIP MANIA

Although the tulip is thought to have originally come from Turkey, it quickly became very popular in its new adopted home of the Netherlands. During the 17th century, Dutch Golden Age speculators flooded the market, pushing the value of tulips to incredible heights. During this period referred to as "Tulip mania" a single tulip bulb could be worth as much as an Amsterdam townhouse.

Tulip mania reached its peak during the winter of 1636–37. By then, thousands of people—including cobblers, carpenters, bricklayers, and woodcutters—were indulging in frenzied trading. And then, in early February 1637, the market for tulips suddenly collapsed, as even the cheapest bulbs had become too expensive for most speculators. Demand crashed and tulips tumbled to a tenth of their former values. The result was financial catastrophe for many.

A Satire of Tulip Mania by Jan Brueghel the Younger (ca. 1640) depicts speculators as brainless monkeys in contemporary upper–class dress.

Amsterdam
Dam Square
ca. 1890

WWII

The Netherlands was invaded on 10th May 1940 by Nazi Germany. The Dutch government and royal family were rushed to the relative safety of England; however, the country suffered greatly, losing approximately 200,000 citizens throughout the war. The Netherlands was finally liberated on 5th May 1945 by allied forces.

DUTCH FAMINE

During the late stages of the war, the Netherlands was unable to secure enough food as they were cut off from supplies by the German blockade. The winter of 1944 was exceptionally harsh and is known as 'Hunger Winter' due to the famine that ravaged the country (around 22,000 people are thought to have died as a result of the famine). The Dutch rallied together and created soup kitchens in order to feed as many people as possible.

– 3 –
Highlights

Today Amsterdam is a beautiful, bustling city that has become one of the top tourist destinations in the world. From its Golden Age history to its modern architecture, its state–of–the–art museums and thriving cultural scene, Amsterdam has something to offer everyone. Let's have a look at the top must–see highlights this city has to offer.

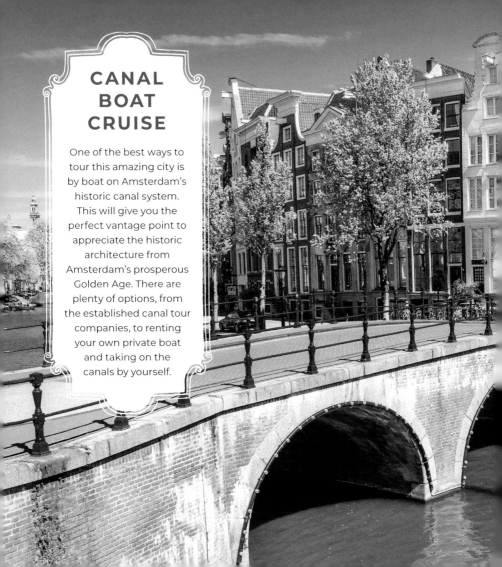

CANAL BOAT CRUISE

One of the best ways to tour this amazing city is by boat on Amsterdam's historic canal system. This will give you the perfect vantage point to appreciate the historic architecture from Amsterdam's prosperous Golden Age. There are plenty of options, from the established canal tour companies, to renting your own private boat and taking on the canals by yourself.

RIJKSMUSEUM

The Rijksmuseum holds art from the middle ages onwards, which makes it a varied and historically diverse museum. Its collections of European and Asian art include various mediums such as paintings, statues, glassware, metalwork, and even furniture. The museum holds a large proportion of portraits from all ages with biblical scenes, still life, and landscapes.

THE NIGHT-WATCH

The Night Watch by Rembrandt was commissioned around 1639 and portrays a militia company captained by Frans Banning Cocq. Rembrandt used several different painting techniques: there is intricate detail in parts of the picture, where other parts are textured with layers of paint. There is plenty of symbolism to be had within. *The Night Watch* used to be coated with a dark varnish, giving the incorrect impression that the painting depicted a night scene (hence the name). The varnish was finally removed in the 1940s.

THE MILKMAID

The Milkmaid has a place of pride
in Amsterdam's Rijksmuseum. The
oil painting was completed in 1658
by Johannes Vermeer and depicts
a servant pouring milk from a jug
into a bowl on a table laden with
food. The scene is simple but the
contrast between the maid and
table with her surroundings is stark.
The subject comes across as a
virtuous, wholesome woman of low
ranking through its understated and
simplistic scenario. If you look closely,
Cupid is hidden amongst the tiles.

VAN GOGH MUSEUM

The Van Gogh Museum is where you will find the vast majority of Vincent van Gogh's masterpieces. The museum opened in 1973 after the Vincent van Gogh Foundation took control of the collection. Having not had much success during his lifetime, van Gogh might be pleased to know his work is being shown to an ever increasing amount of visitors with over two million in 2016. The permanent collection includes the infamous *Sunflowers*, as well as work by Monet and other artists.

VINCENT VAN GOGH

Vincent Willem van Gogh was born in 1853. During his lifetime he painted over two thousand works. His unique post–impressionist style is so particular to him that his work is easily recognisable with its visible brush strokes and dramatic assembly. Van Gogh grew up in the Netherlands and eventually moved to London to train as an art dealer. He also spent time in Belgium and Paris where he drew on the scenery and fellow artists for further inspiration.

Van Gogh was a deeply religious man (and was even a pastor for a short time) but suffered from melancholy throughout his life. Van Gogh died in 1890 after suffering his entire adult years with mental health that included the infamous removal of his ear. During his lifetime he was not considered successful by any means but drew continued acclaim upwardly after his death.He is now considered one of the most famous artists of his time.

THE BEDROOM IN ARLES

This series of three paintings were originally named *The Bedroom* and depicted Van Gogh's own bedroom during his time in Arles, France. The first version was painted in 1888 and the second and third in 1889. Each version recreates the same scene but with differing vibrancy, warmth, and lighting. Van Gogh painted the initial picture after a time of illness where he was confined to his bed for several days. Later versions were designed for both his mother and sister.

ANNE FRANK HOUSE

Anne Frank was born on 12th June 1929 in Frankfurt, Germany, into a Jewish family. Her father, Otto Frank, moved his business from Germany to Amsterdam in 1940 just after the war began. In hopes of avoiding persecution for being Jewish, Otto created a hideaway within the business premises for himself and his family. In July 1942 they secretly moved into the annex when Margot, Anne's older sister, received a letter stating that she was summoned to join a labour camp.

For just over two years Anne, her family, and another family lived in the cramped space in the annex at the top of the building. It was inside these walls that Anne began her famous diary. She wrote about how the family survived both physically and mentally in their close quarters and about the budding romance she shared with the boy, Peter, who also lived in the annex.

On 4th August 1944 Otto Frank's business and house were searched by the Nazis. Anne and her family and friends, eight people in total, were discovered. The Franks were transported to concentration camps. In October or November 1944, Anne and her sister, Margot, were transferred from Auschwitz to Bergen-Belsen, where they died (probably of typhus) a few months later. Anne was just fifteen years old. Her father was the only survivor in the family and he went on to recover Anne's beloved diary and later to publish its contents, enabling Anne Frank's story to survive.

VONDELPARK

Vondelpark, named after the 17th–century
playwright and poet, is the most popular
park in Amsterdam and with its 120 acres
of land, it has plenty to offer. An open–air
theatre and three restaurants are situated
in the park. You can even hire a set of skates
and join the weekly Friday 'skate night'.
There are said to be around 70 different
species of roses blooming on its lush
grounds.

HEINEKEN BROUWER

ntrumring s 100

HEINEKEN EXPERIENCE

The Heineken brewery was established in Amsterdam in 1864 as a local family business. The brewery's historic building, no longer in use as an actual brewery, has now been turned into a museum and adult amusement park. Needless to say, there are tasters available in the bar and exhibits highlighting the beer making business including photographs, original brewing equipment, and interactive multimedia displays.

ALFRED 'FREDDY' HENRY HEINEKEN
worldly

ALFRED 'FREDDY' HENRY HEINEKEN

FREDDY HEINEKEN

Freddy Heineken was the CEO of the Heineken International brewing company, a family business, and one of the richest men in the Netherlands. In 1983 both himself and his driver were kidnapped by three armed men and held for a ransom of 35 million Dutch guilders. The perpetrators were eventually found and arrested but not before Freddy and his driver had endured a horrific three–week ordeal. There have been many books written and two movies made about the crime, the most recent in 2015 starring Anthony Hopkins.

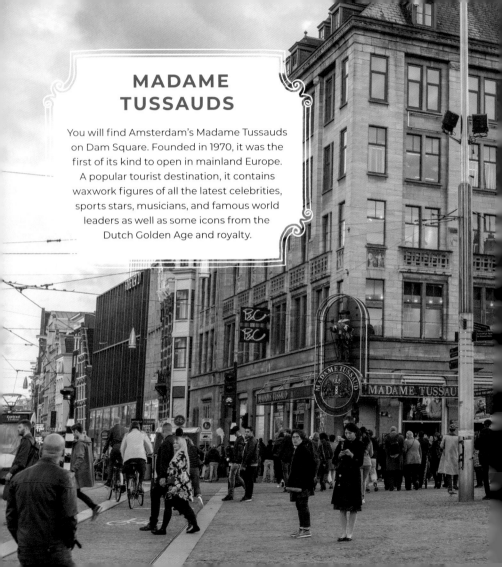

MADAME TUSSAUDS

You will find Amsterdam's Madame Tussauds on Dam Square. Founded in 1970, it was the first of its kind to open in mainland Europe. A popular tourist destination, it contains waxwork figures of all the latest celebrities, sports stars, musicians, and famous world leaders as well as some icons from the Dutch Golden Age and royalty.

A'DAM TOWER

This 22–story building was built in 1970 by
the Royal Dutch Shell Oil Company but has
recently been refurbished into a modern
night–life venue. The tower consists of
restaurants, nightclubs, and a hotel. It also
boasts a fantastic look–out gallery with
a swing that reaches over the edge of
the tower, giving the bravest of people a
spectacular view of the city.

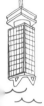

ARTIS ZOO

The Artis Zoo was founded in 1838 and now receives 1.3 million visitors every year. It consists of stunning listed buildings which have been recently renovated, a wide array of animals, birds, insects, and playgrounds as well as a restaurant–solarium.

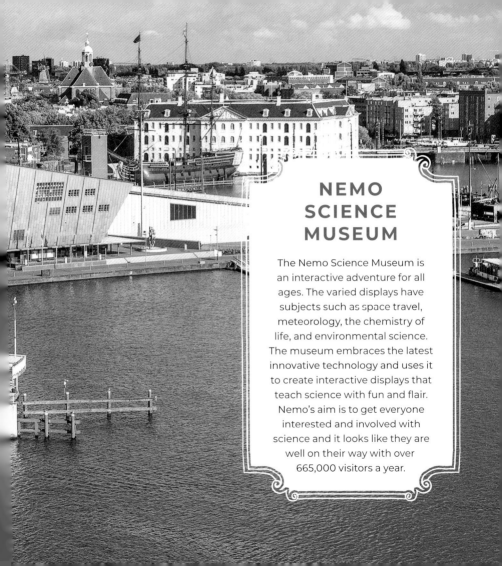

NEMO
SCIENCE
MUSEUM

The Nemo Science Museum is an interactive adventure for all ages. The varied displays have subjects such as space travel, meteorology, the chemistry of life, and environmental science. The museum embraces the latest innovative technology and uses it to create interactive displays that teach science with fun and flair. Nemo's aim is to get everyone interested and involved with science and it looks like they are well on their way with over 665,000 visitors a year.

– 4 –

Neighbour-hoods

Amsterdam has a variety of neighbourhoods—each with different characters and a charm of their own. Take a walk and explore the cafés, restaurants and other highlights each area has to offer.

OLD CITY CENTER

The historic city center of Amsterdam is host to renowned museums, charming and high-end shopping areas, vibrant markets, fantastic culture and entertainment.

TOP must sees:

1. Dam square
2. Red Light District
3. Nieuwmarkt
4. Kalverstraat shopping area
5. Flower market

DAM SQUARE

Dam Square and its plaza are packed full of interesting sights. It was the original site of the dam over the river Amstel and the town grew around it slowly, forming the city you see today. Within the square, you will find Madame Tussauds, the 15th century Gothic New Church (Nieuwe Kerk), and the Royal Palace. Several tram lines cross the square and you will see that it is a popular meeting place for people as well as a place of historic importance.

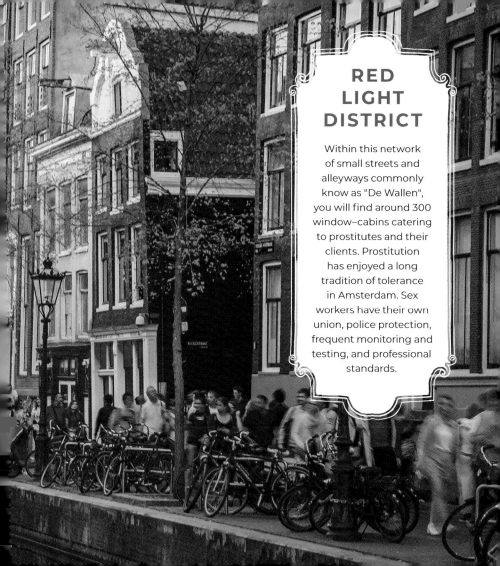

RED LIGHT DISTRICT

Within this network of small streets and alleyways commonly know as "De Wallen", you will find around 300 window–cabins catering to prostitutes and their clients. Prostitution has enjoyed a long tradition of tolerance in Amsterdam. Sex workers have their own union, police protection, frequent monitoring and testing, and professional standards.

NIEUW-MARKT

The Nieuwmarkt sits next to the red light district within Amsterdam's China Town. It still houses various weekly markets and the neighbouring streets are lined with shops, cafés and restaurants. It is a great place to find antique books and organic homegrown produce. In the 1970s there were plans to tear it down in favour of a road but the locals saved the market and it still stands in the historic setting beside what was once a medieval gateway.

KALVER-STRAAT

Kalverstraat roughly translates to Calf Street and is one of the busiest shopping streets in Amsterdam. It is a place of great historic importance. In 1345 a miracle was said to have happened in a house in Kalverstraat and a chapel now sits on that very spot. It is also the site of several tragedies: at the end of WWII where 19 civilians lost their lives and again in 1977 when 33 people were killed in a fire.

FLOWER MARKET

The flower market (Bloemenmarkt) was founded in 1862 and is the only floating market in the world. The market is set on floating barges and the flowers are often brought in via the canals. The market holds stalls from florists, and gardening shops selling anything from cut flowers and bulbs to seedlings and equipment. It is one of the most beautiful markets in Europe and possibly the most fragrant.

50 Tulpen
€ 12.50

DE SLUYSWACHT

This historic building has seen many uses but now it is a local café and is enjoyed by many. It began life in 1695 as a lockhouse, which is a house for the person who controls and manages the lock adjacent to the building. Situated in Sint Antoniessluis, it provides a scenic backdrop for a drink by the water. It has retained its charm and character throughout its long existence and is a wonderful example of late 17th–century architecture.

PORTUGUESE SYNAGOGUE

The Portuguese synagogue was built in 1675 and is one of the largest in the world. During the Dutch Golden Age, the Jewish community, particularly the Sephardic community, were a large and prosperous group as seen by the grandeur of the synagogue. The floor was designed to be covered in sand in order to muffle the sound of footsteps and it is one of only five synagogues in the world that uses sand flooring.

REMBRANDT HOUSE

Rembrandt's house and workshop have been restored and form the basis of this intriguing museum. Within its walls are not only sketches and paintings from Rembrandt's collection but also an inside view of his home life and working conditions. Rembrandt's illustrious history is retold including his downfall and ultimate bankruptcy in 1658. Over his lifetime, Rembrandt painted around three hundred pictures along with hundreds of sketches and drawings. Many of them are displayed in the museum along with pieces from Rembrandt's tutor, pupils, and fellow artists.

REMBRANDT VAN RIJN

Rembrandt was born in 1606 and although he is mostly known for his paintings, he was also an accomplished draughtsman and printmaker. His career took place in the height of the Dutch Golden Age in which Dutch art was highly popular and sought after. His work consists primarily of portraits, landscapes, biblical scenes, and animal studies, although he was adept at all genres. He was highly acclaimed and admired by other artists for his classic style with Italian influence.

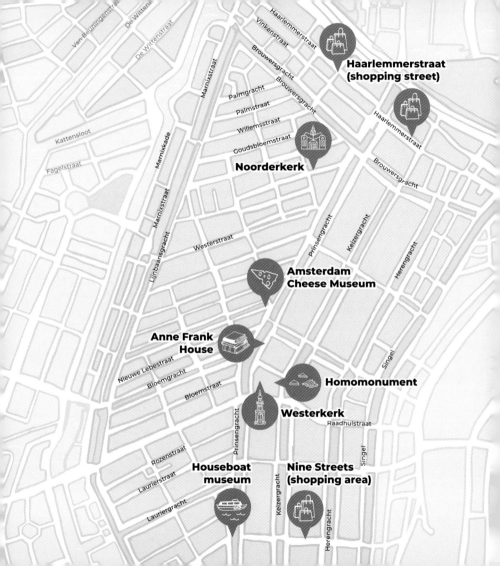

**Haarlemmerstraat
(shopping street)**

Haarlemmerstraat

Noorderkerk

**Amsterdam
Cheese Museum**

**Anne Frank
House**

Homomonument

Westerkerk

**Houseboat
museum**

**Nine Streets
(shopping area)**

JORDAAN

The Jordaan neighbourhood is bordered by the Singelgracht canal and has gone from being a working class area to a more affluent and vibrant place to live and work. The area contains many art galleries and actually housed Rembrandt during the latter part of his life. The district is also famous for being the location of the Anne Frank House which sits on the edge of the Prisengracht canal.

TOP must sees:

1. Nine streets (Negen straatjes)
2. Anne Frank house
3. Westerkerk
4. Westerpark
5. Haarlemmerstraat

NINE STREETS

The Nine Streets (negen straatjes) is an informal designation for an area of Amsterdam consisting of nine delightful boutique–filled streets. The area boasts several unique shops which include vintage and designer brands, cafés, restaurants, and bars. The Nine Streets has an old town, Bohemian air and is the perfect place to spend an afternoon.

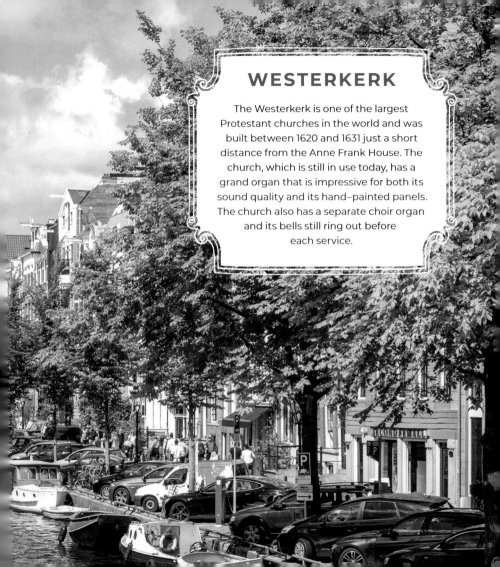

WESTERKERK

The Westerkerk is one of the largest Protestant churches in the world and was built between 1620 and 1631 just a short distance from the Anne Frank House. The church, which is still in use today, has a grand organ that is impressive for both its sound quality and its hand–painted panels. The church also has a separate choir organ and its bells still ring out before each service.

View from the bell
tower of the Westerkerk
(Westertoren)

WESTERPARK

Amsterdam's Westerpark is a vibrant expanse of green space within a lively district. There's always plenty of action whether in the form of street markets, boutiques, cinemas, theatres, or cozy local pubs and restaurants.

HAARLEMMERSTRAAT

The Haarlemmerstraat is situated on top of the Jordaan district and is home to a wide array of shops, bars, and restaurants. It's the perfect place to unwind and even houses Amsterdam's oldest cinema.

Rembrandtplein

Herr
Mus

Handbag
Museum

FOAM
Museum

Herengracht

Magere Brug

Museum
van Loon

Kerkstraat

Keizergracht

Prinsengracht

Kerkstraat

Prinsengracht

Amstel

Vijzelgracht

Noorderstraat

Nieuwe Loolersstraat

Rijksmuseum

I amsterdam Sign

Heineken
Experience

Hemonylaan

Albert Cuyp Market

Tweede Jan Steenstraat

Govert Flinckstraat

Jan Steenstraat

DE PIJP & EASTERN CANAL RING

De Pijp is a Bohemian neighbourhood full of diverse restaurants, pubs, cafés, and markets. The Eastern Canal Ring offers you a view of what the Dutch Golden Age left behind. Sumptuous buildings with stunning architecture line the streets. Don't miss the Museum of Bags and Purses tucked along the Herengracht.

TOP must sees:

1. Albert Cuyp Markt
2. Heineken Experience
3. Rembrandt Square
4. Hermitage
5. Museum van Loon

ALBERT CUYP MARKT

This market, situated in the De Pijp district, is the largest in all of the Netherlands and is open six days a week. The market began in 1912 and sells anything from food to household wares. There are stalls with exotic goods, fresh fruit and vegetables. Lining the market are plenty of bars, cafés, and restaurants to keep shoppers refreshed.

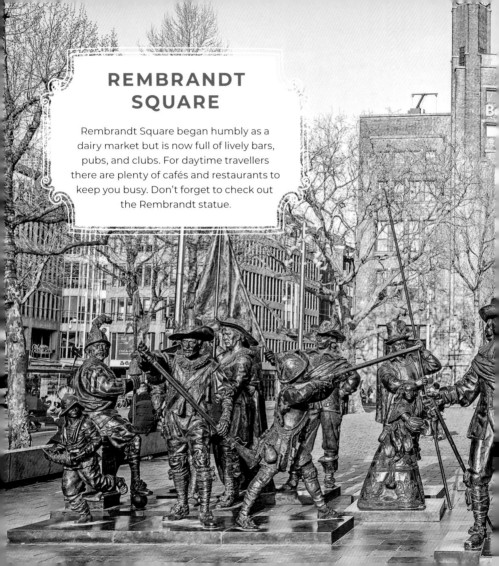

REMBRANDT SQUARE

Rembrandt Square began humbly as a dairy market but is now full of lively bars, pubs, and clubs. For daytime travellers there are plenty of cafés and restaurants to keep you busy. Don't forget to check out the Rembrandt statue.

HERMITAGE MUSEUM

The Hermitage Museum is situated alongside the Amstel river. The building dates from 1681 although it only became a museum in 2007. Inside it is fully equipped with the latest technology to care for its extensive collection of paintings and statues. The museum, a branch of the Hermitage Museum based in Saint Petersburg, Russia, also houses a restaurant and lecture halls.

The Magere Brug
(Skinny bridge)

Kinkerstraat

Derde Helmersstraat

Leidsekade

Leidseplein

Rijksmus

Jacob Van Lennepkade

aalstraat

helminastraat

Brederodestraat

Eerste Helmersstraat

Zandpad

Vossiusstraat

Vondelstraat

Van Gogh Museum

P.C. Hooftstraat

a

I amsterdam Sig

Vondelpark

Van Eeghenlaan

Stedelijk Museum

Van Eeghenstraat

Museumsquare

Van Breestraat

Valeriusstraat

Johannes Verhulststraat

De Lairessestraat

OLD SOUTH

Oud Zuid is a posh corner of the city that is
well-established, and contains some of the
most elegant buildings and beautiful parks
including Vondelpark and Museum Square.
The area was developed predominantly
at the end of the 19th century and you will
find many of Amsterdam's most affluent
dwellings along its leafy streets.

TOP must sees:

1. Museum square (Rijks/Van Gogh & Stedelijk museum)
2. I amsterdam Letters
3. Vondelpark
4. P.C. Hooftstraat
5. Leidseplein

MUSEUM SQUARE

Museum Square is where you will find three of Amsterdam's major museums: the Rijksmuseum, the Van Gogh Museum, and the Stedelijk Museum. The square began life as marshland and then a candle factory but was redeveloped into a town square in the late 1800s.

STEDELIJK MUSEUM

The Stedelijk Museum is located in Museum Square and focuses on contemporary and modern art. It first opened in 1895 and contains work from artists such as Van Gogh, Pollock, and Warhol. The building's original structure was built in the Dutch neo–Renaissance style but has recently been restored and adorned with a spacious additional wing referred to as "the bathtub". The museum houses a library, restaurant, and auditorium.

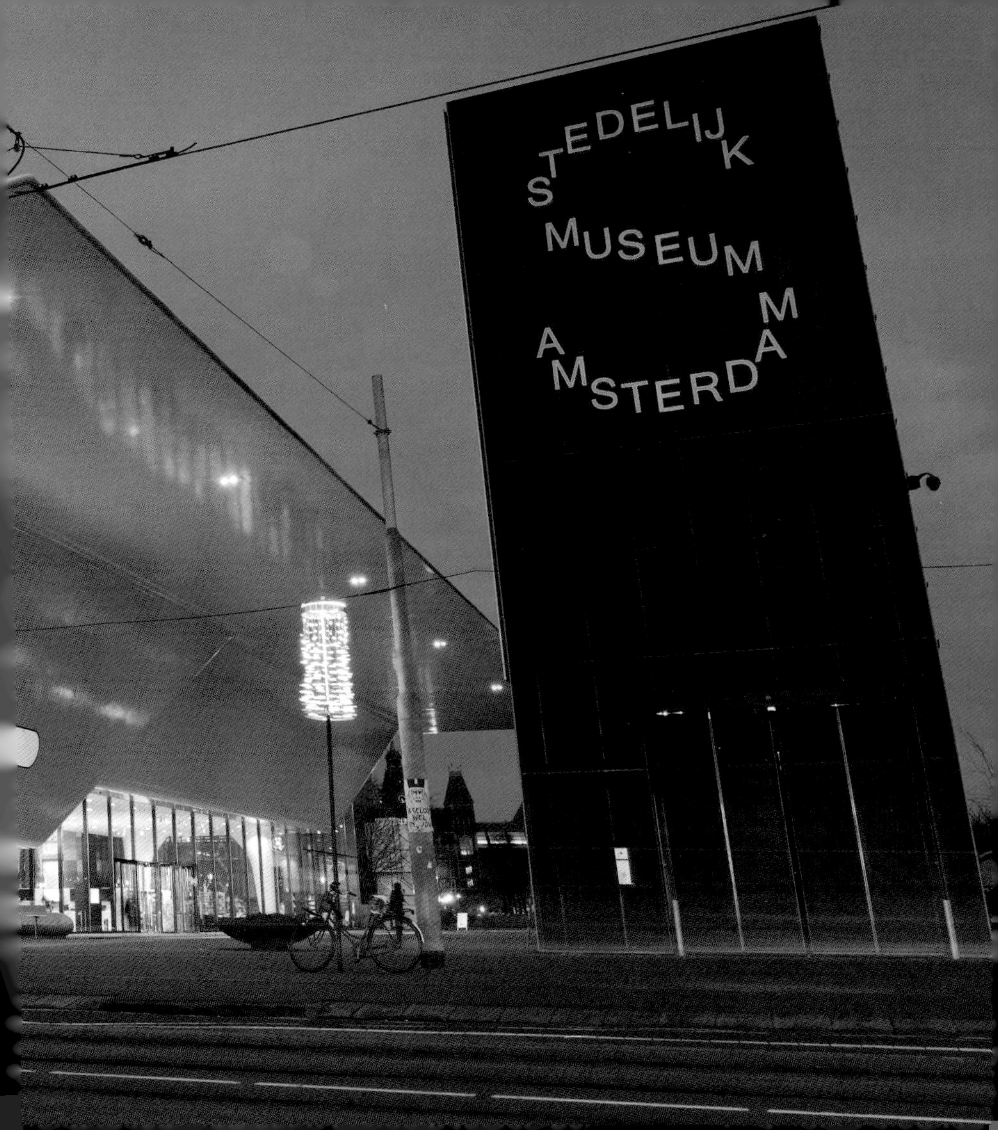
STEDELIJK
MUSEUM
AMSTERDAM

Wall Drawing #1084
by Sol LeWitt

P.C. HOOFTSTRAAT

This posh highstreet stocks all the major luxury brands and designers. The street was named after a Dutch poet, playwright, and historian, Pieter Corneliszoon Hooft, who lived during the Golden Age.

LEIDSEPLEIN

This busy square is next to the Vondelpark and it is a popular place for those looking for a good night out on the town.

THE
I AMSTERDAM
LETTERS

These can be found at the rear of the Rijksmuseum and have become an enormously popular place to have your photograph taken while visiting the capital. The letters are over 2m tall and 23.5m long and you will find visitors perched on them night and day.

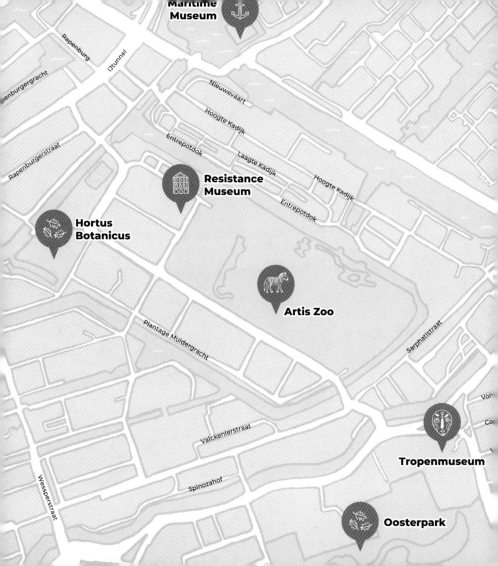

AMSTERDAM OOST (EAST)

Amsterdam Oost has a population of over 123,000 and is an up and coming neighbourhood. In this area of Amsterdam you will find shopping centres, schools, and colleges among the 19th–century dwellings and businesses, not to mention a few of the most popular museums. The majestic Artis Zoo and Hortus are a must see. Oh, and don't forget the fantastic Oosterpark.

TOP must sees:

1. Artis
2. Oosterpark
3. Tropenmuseum
4. Maritime museum
5. Hortus

OOSTERPARK

Oosterpark was the first large park designed by the municipality of Amsterdam. It was created in 1891 to be just like an English garden. The park contains a beautiful large pond, a memorial to Theo van Gogh as well as The National Slavery Monument, which commemorates the abolition of slavery in the Netherlands in 1863.

TROPENMUSEUM

The Tropenmuseum is all about people. It celebrates human nature in all diversities, from all cultures and from many different aspects. The museum contains 340,000 pieces of art: 175,000 are objects such as sculptures and paintings and 155,000 are photographic. The pieces document humanity in historic and cultural settings and portray emotional content such as grief, joy, relationships, and beliefs as well as physical aspects such as fashion, ornamentation and body image.

NATIONAL MARITIME MUSEUM

The museum is situated near the old city harbour and was originally built in 1656 but it was recently renovated to include a glass structure which encloses the courtyard. The space is lit in the evenings to create a starry sky overhead. The quay immediately outside the museum boasts a large replica of the three–masted ship *The Amsterdam* which was part of the Dutch East India Company. Visitors are able to board the ship and explore the close confines within.

Moored just outside the museum is a replica of the *Amsterdam*, an 18th–century ship which sailed between the Netherlands and the East Indies.Have a look inside!

HORTUS

Hortus is a beautiful botanical centre which includes gardens, glass structures, an orangery, and a café. Opened in 1638, it was designed to provide doctors with herbs and plants for healing tinctures and medicines. Today you can find a vast collection of rare plants and trees from distant lands.

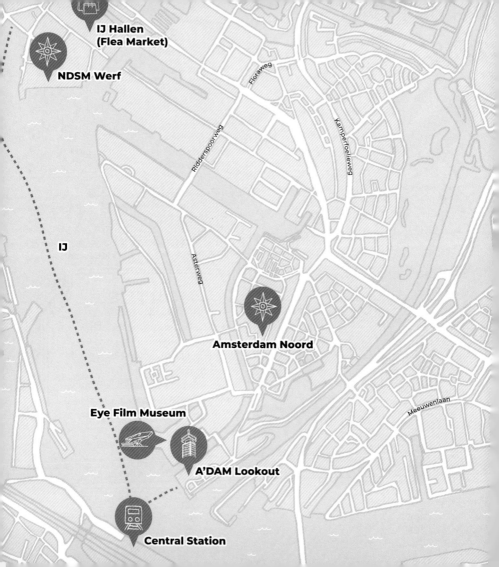

IJ Hallen
(Flea Market)

NDSM Werf

Floraweg

Ridderspoorweg

Kamperfoelieweg

IJ

Asterweg

Amsterdam Noord

Meeuwenlaan

Eye Film Museum

A'DAM Lookout

Central Station

AMSTERDAM NOORD (NORTH)

Amsterdam Noord is separated from Amsterdam Centrum by the IJ which is a body of water that was once a bay. It is a stylish area with plenty of modern architecture including the new A'DAM tower. It is linked to the Amsterdam Centrum by a bridge, tunnels, ferries, and a soon–to–be metro line.

TOP must sees:

1. EYE film museum
2. A'DAM lookout
3. NDSM werf
4. IJ Hallen (flea market)
5. Free ferry rides

EYE FILM MUSEUM

This modern iconic building was opened in 2012. It houses a museum, cinema, and café and sits on the bank of the river IJ. The building holds the latest exhibitions of art and contains film collections in its vast archives using state–of–the–art technology to protect the volatile materials. Some of the film in the archives dates back from the late 1800s.

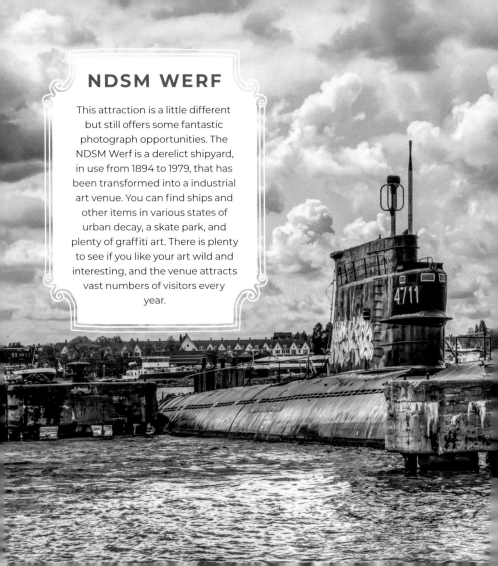

NDSM WERF

This attraction is a little different but still offers some fantastic photograph opportunities. The NDSM Werf is a derelict shipyard, in use from 1894 to 1979, that has been transformed into a industrial art venue. You can find ships and other items in various states of urban decay, a skate park, and plenty of graffiti art. There is plenty to see if you like your art wild and interesting, and the venue attracts vast numbers of visitors every year.

IJ HALLEN

This flea market is one of the biggest in Europe with around 750 stands and is a fantastic place to grab a bargain whether you are looking for clothes, furniture, or something a little different. Located in Amsterdam Noord, it is well worth a visit.

- 5 -

Festivities

Amsterdam has many festivities and the Dutch like to celebrate things with style all year round.

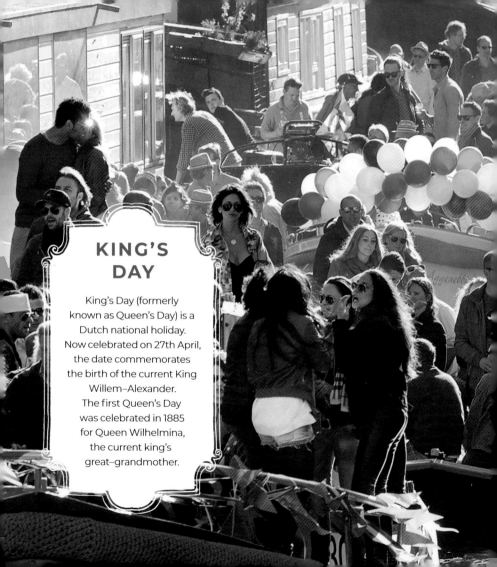

KING'S DAY

King's Day (formerly known as Queen's Day) is a Dutch national holiday. Now celebrated on 27th April, the date commemorates the birth of the current King Willem–Alexander. The first Queen's Day was celebrated in 1885 for Queen Wilhelmina, the current king's great–grandmother.

Orange is the national colour of the Netherlands and therefore all of Amsterdam turns orange on King's Day. There are lots of fun things to do during the day for the whole family and the canals are full to bursting point with colourfully decorated barges.

On King's Day you will find that the whole city has turned into the largest flea market in the world. Everyone is entitled to set up a stall and start selling. So it's a great time to grab a bargain or earn yourself some extra cash. The streets will be filled with goodies.

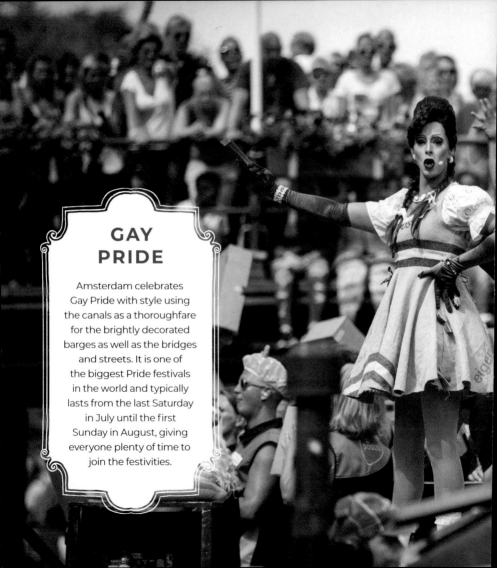

GAY PRIDE

Amsterdam celebrates Gay Pride with style using the canals as a thoroughfare for the brightly decorated barges as well as the bridges and streets. It is one of the biggest Pride festivals in the world and typically lasts from the last Saturday in July until the first Sunday in August, giving everyone plenty of time to join the festivities.

SAIL
AMSTERDAM

Sail Amsterdam began in 1975 to celebrate the 700th anniversary of the city of Amsterdam. Tall ships from every corner of the globe travel to Amsterdam to join in the event and moor at IJhaven where they can be viewed and sometimes boarded. It is one of the biggest maritime events in the world.

AMSTERDAM LIGHT FESTIVAL

Amsterdam light festival is a visually stunning festival that takes place every winter. Many artists come from afar to showcase their unique light designs which they install across Amsterdam's bridges, waterways and public spaces. Parts of the city turn into a fairy–lit wonderland drawing many visitors to see the spectacle.

SINTERKLAAS

Sinterklaas (Saint Nicholas) is not unlike Santa Clause but this Dutch version came first and is celebrated with a feast and the giving of presents on St Nicholas' Eve (5th December).

CHRISTMAS

Christmas is a special time in Amsterdam no matter your religious beliefs. Experience the romance of the city and its canals, decked out in beautiful Christmas lights. Head out into the shopping areas to find the perfect gift, take in a classical concert or ballet performance, or explore the special routes of the Amsterdam Light Festival.

NEW YEAR'S EVE

New Year's Eve for the Dutch is usually spent having fun with family and friends, watching the countless firework displays, or partying into the early hours.

OLIEBOLLEN

Oliebollen roughly translates into "oily balls" and are a delicious holiday treat. Deep fried doughballs are coated in powdered sugar and eaten while still warm. You will find these traditional doughnut–style treats on stalls in the streets.

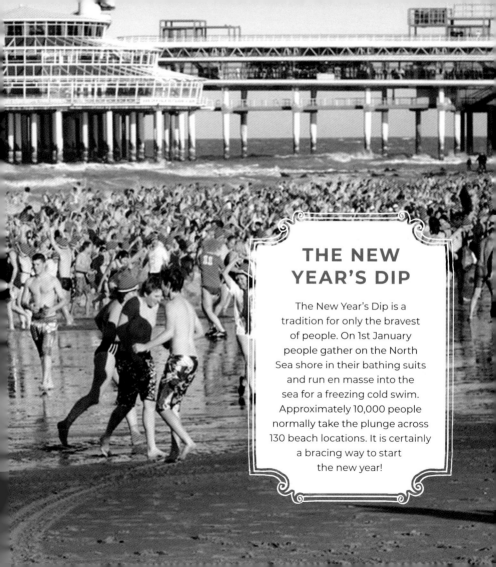

THE NEW YEAR'S DIP

The New Year's Dip is a tradition for only the bravest of people. On 1st January people gather on the North Sea shore in their bathing suits and run en masse into the sea for a freezing cold swim. Approximately 10,000 people normally take the plunge across 130 beach locations. It is certainly a bracing way to start the new year!

- 6 -

Beyond the city

There's plenty to see beyond Amsterdam. With stunning countryside views, historic buildings, and quaint villages the Amsterdam area should not be missed!

KEUKENHOF

Sometimes known as the "Garden of Europe", Keukenhof contains over 32 hectares of parkland bursting with coloured blooms and sweet scents. In 1949 the Mayor of Lisse established the gardens as a place for Dutch growers to exhibit their hybrid flowers to boost the flower export industry. Keukenhof Gardens are a stunning sight to see and are best viewed between March and May.

ZAANSE SCHANS

Zaanse Schans is a scenic district containing a historic collection of well preserved windmills, warehouses, and workshops. It is an area of historic industrial significance and a stunning sight to see. There are several dwellings and businesses that have been turned into museums alongside over 75,000 local residents. It is a perfect place for a unique photographic opportunity and an iconic sight just a short distance from Amsterdam.

VOLENDAM

Volendam is a beautiful town north east of Amsterdam. It boasts colourful wooden houses and old fishing boats, making it a picturesque village full of history. Volendam has its own museum which contains original artifacts and costumes from surrounding areas. It is most definitely a must see.

Get a photo taken of you and your family in traditional Voldendam costumes!

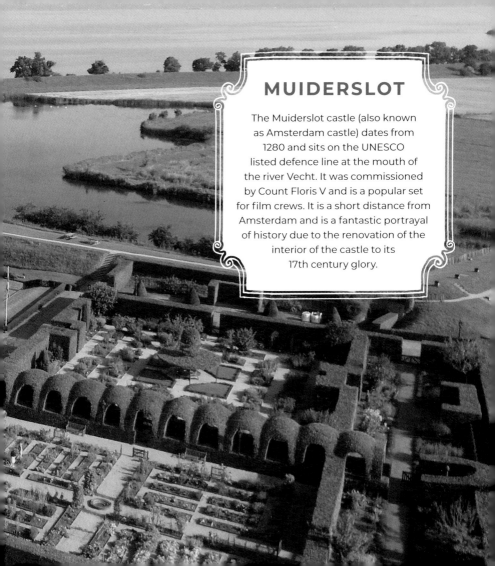

MUIDERSLOT

The Muiderslot castle (also known as Amsterdam castle) dates from 1280 and sits on the UNESCO listed defence line at the mouth of the river Vecht. It was commissioned by Count Floris V and is a popular set for film crews. It is a short distance from Amsterdam and is a fantastic portrayal of history due to the renovation of the interior of the castle to its 17th century glory.

AMSTERDAM BEACH

Amsterdam has some stunning beaches only a hop, skip and a jump from the city centre. Long stretches of flat sandy coastline make these Dutch beaches perfect for watersports, sun bathing, and nightlife. Visit the sandy dunes or spend the day wind surfing. These beaches are some of the most unspoilt in Europe, making them perfect for any activity.

ABOUT US

Stuff Dutch People Like is a celebration of all things Dutch. Started as a simple blog back in 2011, the Stuff Dutch People Like community now boasts a loyal following of over a half million fans in the Netherlands and around the world! The original Stuff Dutch People Like book was published in 2013 and became an instant international bestseller, with other books following suit! Visit us at **www.stuffdutchpeoplelike.com**

OUR BESTSELLING BOOKSERIES

From the creators of the best-selling Stuff Dutch People Like series comes this new and humorous guide to what really makes Dutch people so very... Dutch. This hilarious read will have you nodding your head in agreement - and might just have you wiping away tears of laughter!

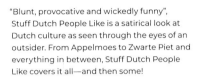

"Blunt, provocative and wickedly funny", Stuff Dutch People Like is a satirical look at Dutch culture as seen through the eyes of an outsider. From Appelmoes to Zwarte Piet and everything in between, Stuff Dutch People Like covers it all—and then some!

From the creators of Stuff Dutch People Like comes this hilarious companion. Stuff Dutch People Say delves deep into the linguistic world of the Lowlands, exploring what happens when Dutch and English collide. From funny Dutch words, incomprehensible Dutch expressions and hysterical examples of Dunglish, we've got you covered!

Stuff Dutch People Eat is a comprehensive celebration of Dutch cuisine. Whether you're looking for festive sweets, traditional tastes or colonial classics, we've got something for every appetite! From breakfast straight through to dessert, Stuff Dutch People Eat will lead you through a culinary adventure spanning flavours— and centuries!

Stuff Dutch Moms Like investigates why Dutch moms are amongst the happiest in the world—and how they manage to have it all! Filled with hilarious anecdotes, tips and tricks, Stuff Dutch Moms Like takes an inside look at parenting in the Netherlands and the secrets to raising the happiest children in the world!

246

247